The "IEPs for Children with Special Needs" Series:

How to Navigate the Minefield of Laws and Rules (Book 1)

DAVID SOFI

The "IEPs for Children with Special Needs" Series: How to Navigate the Minefield of Laws and Rules (Book 1)

Copyright © 2020 by David Sofi

ISBN-13: 978-1-7346555-1-3

Cover creation by Ravi Verma from rdezines

Editing and formatting by Lorraine Reguly from www.WordingWell.com

Dedication

This book and its series is dedicated to the loving memory of my wife and soulmate, Ellie, who gave me the strength and courage to carry on.

This series is also dedicated to YOU and to all the caring parents and guardians of our children who need helping hands.

Table of Contents

Introduction

Imagine walking into a school room crowded with teachers, therapists, district officials, a psychologist, and maybe even a lawyer. You are there to represent your special needs child. You don't know what to expect, what everyone will say, or what they will ask you. Your stomach is churning, your palms are sweaty, and you feel as though you might throw up at any minute.

You need to feel powerful and confident.

I am about to help you get that confidence.

Power and confidence come from having the knowledge and the understanding of the Federal Laws written to help and protect your student-child in the educational system.

You will breathe more easily and feel less frightened. Get ready for me to share with you the hard-won lessons I learned from walking through and surviving the mountains and valleys of government red-tape. I will help you navigate the minefield of laws and rules surrounding your special needs child's IEP (Individualized Education Program).

You need to know your rights ahead of time, before the meeting. You can't do this in the spur of the moment. It's your child, there's too much emotion, there are too many issues to discuss, and there is not enough time to catch up when facing such an audience.

Knowledge is power. The more knowledge you have, the more power and confidence you will have. Unless you are an attorney or a Special Education teacher, you need this power to be in your child's IEP team meeting as an equal member of the group that includes professional teachers, therapists, school officials, psychologists, and maybe even a school district attorney.

This book is the first in a series that makes special education laws understandable for parents.

We'll deal with the basics in Book 1. In Books 2 and 3, we'll delve into more specialized questions and areas. Each chapter of each book will have three parts: an overview, an explanation, and a summary checklist of the key points mentioned in that chapter.

This series will help you immensely, by giving you the knowledge and confidence you need. It will also help you ensure that your child receives the best education possible.

Individualized Educational Programs (IEPs) and the Federal Education Law

"They have no lawyers among them, for they consider them as a sort of people whose profession it is to disguise matters." —from Sir Thomas More's book, Utopia.

It seems that lawyers, especially those who write laws, are intent on disguising matters. It seems it takes a law degree to read and understand those laws. And it seems to take a lawyer who specializes in Federal Education Law to understand IEPs.

But don't worry. My job is to translate the key points of the law into understandable language. I will arm you with the knowledge you need to become powerful in managing your child's IEP.

Your child's IEP because it is a contract that spells out how the school must help your child learn and graduate from high school.

Your child's education is essential for many reasons. An education can help your child communicate better. It can open opportunities for employment. An education can help your child learn to feed and dress themselves, and how to manage money. It can teach appropriate behavior in social settings. It can help your child grow into a self-sufficient adult. The most important reason is the promise and expectation of a better and more successful life, upon graduation.

It can also take a huge burden off your shoulders.

The school must provide this help to you for free. The IEP is your guarantee your child will receive what is needed to help him or her learn and graduate.

Every child in America is guaranteed a free, appropriate, public school education (FAPE)... all the way through high school. It is a Federal Law. If your child's disability or special need interferes with learning in a regular classroom, with regular teaching methods, then the school must adapt to your child.

One way to adapt is through an IEP—an Individualized Education Program. This is a program that is customized to your child's needs.

It will not be an "off-the-rack, one size fits all" thing. However, you should not expect the schools to volunteer to provide everything your child needs or deserves.

Even if school officials and employees want to help your child, and most do, they don't know your child as well as you do, they won't think of everything, and they have budgets to protect.

IEPs are there to help your child, but you have to get in the driver's seat. You need to lead the way to get your child the contract they need and deserve.

We all know that education is the key to independent living, to getting and keeping meaningful jobs, and to knowing how to raise a healthy family. We all know that school isn't just about reading, writing, and arithmetic. Students without disabilities enjoy regular school activities such as sports, physical education, band, chorus, art, etc. The law says handicaps aren't excuses for not providing these same activities—as appropriate—to children with special needs.

Does this mean a child in a wheelchair must be allowed to join the football team? No. That wouldn't be appropriate.

But must the school ensure that same student can attend football games with classmates? Yes, and you can include such activities in your IEP.

I want to make two things clear: 1. I am not an attorney and I am not giving legal advice. 2. There are always exceptions to laws and/or rules. There are always differences of opinions and arguments about what they mean. They were written by lawyers, who would be out of work if the laws and rules were absolute and had no exceptions or interpretations.

Does all this talk about contracts and laws make you nervous? Don't be! My goal is to translate all that legalese into words you understand.

Again, I am not giving legal advice. I am merely translating laws, rules, and regulations, so these matters are not disguised.

"This is the bottom line: teachers affect eternity. They can never tell where their influence stops. A father and mother should be the child's main teachers. You are in charge of your children's education and their future; you truly don't know where your influence will end. Your influence will last for generations." —an excerpt (used with permission) from Bodhi Sanders' book, *Men of the Code: Living as a Superior Man* (p. 135, Kaizen Quest, Kindle Edition)

Let me repeat: get in the driver's seat. You don't need to be a mechanic to drive your car, but you need to know how to drive, how the various buttons and dials work in your car, and the laws that govern your driving. In the same way, to manage your child's IEP, you don't need to know how to teach. You just need to know that you can manage your child's IEP. You know your child better than anyone else in the world. You also need to know enough about the law to know your rights.

I will show you how to drive the IEP process.

I will cover how to know if the IEP is working for your child (and what to do if it isn't).

There are a few very important points to note, up-front:

1) Not every disability qualifies for an IEP. The disability must also interfere with successful learning in school.

2) In its simplest form, maybe your child can learn, but just not fast enough to keep up and graduate before reaching 21 years of age. This probably qualifies for an IEP.

3) The IEP is in effect in public schools, through Grade 12. In special situations, it can apply to a private school, but those are special circumstances, which I will cover in another book.

4) An IEP does NOT get your child the very best education possible, nor will it mandate a prep school for Harvard. It only guarantees the resources needed to get the education that children without disabilities get in a public school.

A child may have a limp but may learn just fine. That child may not play school sports but has good grades. School officials will say an IEP isn't justified.

You may prefer a private school on religious grounds. An IEP will not be part of that education, even if your child is handicapped. You, as the parent of such a child, will want to meet with the school officials to discuss how they will accommodate the learning disability, but you won't have the weight of the Federal government behind you.

You may believe in advanced educational techniques used in specialized, private schools. That is not what an IEP is about. The IEP is to "level the playing field" so that a disability does not deprive a child of a "normal" public school education. There may be advanced techniques that magnify the education your child could receive, but as long as your school can provide an appropriate education, you cannot force the IEP into getting more than that.

There can be many reasons a child's grades and progress in school falter or aren't kept up. Congress has said a mental or physical handicap is not an acceptable excuse. Congress has passed laws that say public schools must step up to help level the playing field for those children. Those laws protect the rights to a free and adequate education for those children. The schools must provide the tools needed to overcome the limitations imposed by handicaps and limitations to successfully graduating. And the schools must provide these free to you and your child.

You may feel you need to be a lawyer to read these laws. I felt that way when my special needs granddaughter had to enroll in public school at age three to continue getting her physical, speech, and vision therapy services.

I spent 10 years reading and studying the laws. I paid for training programs in Special Education law. I spent two years getting a Paralegal Diploma.

Now, my goal is to simplify this whole mess and to give you the know-how and skills to be confident your child is getting what is owed to them in school.

Two basic laws have been passed that help and protect children attending schools.

The first is the American with Disabilities Act (ADA), which gives rise to what are called Section 504 plans, designed to prevent discrimination due to disabilities.

The second law is the Individuals with Disabilities Education Act (IDEA), which gives rise to the IEP.

This series of books will translate and simplify the most important things relating to IEPs you will deal with as you navigate through the rough seas of special education.

SUMMARY CHECKLIST:

1. Knowledge is power; the more knowledge you have, the more power you have.

2. Federal Law is your friend, your protector, and your bodyguard, when you go into IEP team meetings.

3. Disabilities are no excuse for a school to avoid providing a free, appropriate, public education.

Chapter 1: What is an IEP?

As I mentioned in the introduction, each chapter of each book will have three parts: an overview, an explanation, and a summary of key points.

OVERVIEW:

The acronym "IEP" stands for "Individualized Education Program."

Let me tell you a secret: an IEP is a unique, one-way contract. You—the parent—are not forced to do anything! Only the school is bound, and it must do whatever is agreed to and written in the IEP. Neither the parent nor the student gives up anything of value for a free, appropriate, public education. You are in the driver's seat! Just as a driver needs a mechanic to keep the car running, you need teachers, therapists, and technology experts. But you are the driver.

An IEP is a one-way contract between you, your child, and the school. It is a one-way contract because it obligates the school to provide specified services and aids (including aides) that will help your child get a free education. You are not obligated to do anything.

Federal Laws enforce this contract for a special education, which is backed up by State Law and your state's department of education rules and procedures. That is a lot of firepower supporting you and your child!

EXPLANATION:

Does "special education" mean placement in a separate classroom for your child?

Absolutely not. In fact, schools must include your child in as much of a "regular" school environment as appropriate.

The days of separating disabled children just because they are disabled are over. They must be included in regular classrooms and school activities, whenever it doesn't interfere with their learning. That means they are included in regular classrooms and outside activities such as sports, field trips, recesses, lunchrooms, and so on.

The key phrase is "as appropriate." Remember, the goal is to meet your child's individual needs. If your child wears leg braces and uses crutches or a wheelchair, playing in basketball games with the other students will likely not happen, but maybe teachers can set up a free-throw competition. If your child is tube-fed, then perhaps lunch won't happen in the cafeteria.

If your child needs one-to-one help from a "shadow" or aide—a person dedicated to helping your student—then a self-contained special education classroom might be better for your child. Remember Helen Keller, the deaf and blind student who graduated from college? She had a shadow throughout school and attended regular classes for much, if not most, of her schooling.

This is a matter for the whole team to discuss and agree upon. That means there is no agreement without you. If you don't agree with the proposed placement in a special education classroom, then you may object, and even refuse.

Decisions about placement are to be made after the child's IEP is developed. You, the parents, are members of the IEP team that decides on placement. Courts have held that schools may not predetermine placement. The team must make the placement decision, and that includes you.

You will hear or read about placing disabled students in the "least restrictive environment" (LRE), or perhaps you will encounter terms like "mainstreaming," "integration," or "full inclusion." This means that students with disabilities should receive their education, as much as is reasonable, with nondisabled students, in regular classrooms. However, if supplemental aids and services are not enough to achieve a satisfactory education in ordinary settings, then special classrooms or settings will be appropriate.

The goal is always to get an appropriate education.

A Section 504 Plan vs. an IEP

A Section 504 Plan (also called an Accommodation Plan) comes from the civil rights law called the Americans with Disabilities Act (ADA).

This Federal Law prohibits discrimination against individuals with disabilities. It applies to a person who will have disabilities for their entire life and is not limited to just schools or education.

An IEP results from the Individuals with Disabilities Act (IDEA) and applies specifically to education from Kindergarten through high school.

IEPs end when the student graduates from high school or reaches the age of 21 (whichever happens first).

IEPs also refer specifically to a public school education, unless the public school does not provide the services or capabilities your child needs to get an appropriate education. In that case, the school district must provide those services or pay for them in a specialized school or institution.

There are some major differences between an IEP and a Section 504 Plan.

In a Section 504 Plan:

◆ Parents have only minimal rights.

◆ Parents don't have to be invited to 504 meetings.

◆ The school does NOT have to prepare a written educational plan.

◆ There are no legal requirements for what should be included in the plan.

◆ The school must provide an "appropriate" education, meaning an education comparable to that provided to students without disabilities, which may include regular or special education services.

◆ Specialized instruction or related services—such as occupational therapy, speech therapy or physical therapy—are not offered through Section 504 Plans.

In an IEP:

◆ Parents must be included in IEP meetings. This means they must be invited to such meetings.

◆ A written plan must be developed, provided to the parents, and followed by the school.

◆ The plan must meet the child's unique needs.

◆ The plan must prepare the child for further education, employment, and independent living.

◆ Parents have many safeguards and protections in place, with the weight of Federal and State governments behind them.

SUMMARY CHECKLIST:

1. An IEP is a one-way contract where the school has all the obligations to adapt and overcome.

2. The law requires placing the student as much as appropriate in regular school classrooms and settings.

3. Parents may refuse or change their minds about receiving special education services under an IEP.

4. Handicapped students may not qualify for an IEP if their grades are not affected by their

disabilities. However, the school is still obligated to accommodate their disabilities—under Section 504 of the ADA—such as providing wheelchair access, Braille supports, and so on.

DAVID SOFI

Chapter 2: How do You Get an IEP?

OVERVIEW:

You don't get or buy your child an IEP.

You must ask to have your child assessed by the school. When you suspect—or know—your child has a learning disability, you can request the school to do an evaluation to determine if your child legally qualifies as having a learning disability.

The school system will provide this for free.

NOTE: You are requesting an evaluation, but you are not yet giving your consent to have your child receive special education and related services. That comes after you get the evaluation report and review and discuss it at an initial team meeting. If the school recommends an IEP, you can accept or refuse it.

Schools have screening programs to identify students who may have learning disabilities. These screening programs are not evaluations, but a screening may turn up signs of a learning handicap.

EXPLANATION:

Teachers may initially ask for an evaluation if they see indications that your child may have a learning disability. However, the school must get your approval for this evaluation before doing it.

The school will contact you and explain what your child's teacher has observed and what the evaluation will include. If you consent to an evaluation, you are not consenting to starting any special education programs or services; you are only giving your go-ahead to do the evaluation.

Can you refuse a special education?

Yes, you can refuse special education services.

Additionally, if you consent to receive special education, you can revoke your consent later. However, you must do that in writing, so you will need to know how to write and submit your revocation. We'll cover that in a later book.

If you stop special education services for your child or refuse such services in the first place, then your child will be a general education student. The school will not need to provide support services such as speech therapy or program accommodations (such as extra time on tests, and so on).

The law does not require the school provide a 504 Plan, although it may voluntarily do so. The ADA laws still protect your child if they have a disability, and their records will always show them as being a person with a disability.

What if a doctor gives my child a medical diagnosis?

A medical diagnosis may replace the need for a formal school assessment.

There are five major diagnoses groups classified in Federal Law as learning disabilities.

If one or more of these applies to your child, then the school district will "rubber stamp" your child as a "Child with Disabilities," and you will move on to the IEP process.

But beware: not all disabilities qualify for an IEP. The child must also "need special education" because of the disability. The school district must agree the disability causes the need.

Congress has declared the following conditions as learning disabilities:

1. Specific Learning Disabilities (SLD), including dyslexia.

2. Hearing disorders (auditory processing disorders).

3. Limited ability to use or understand spoken words (aphasia).

4. Difficulty with handwriting (dysgraphia), including illegible writing, awkward pencil grip, abnormal sized or spaced letters, and spelling problems.

5. Difficulty with math (dyscalculia).

6. Motor control problems (dyspraxia), such as large motor or fine motor lack of control. The child may have difficulty with their hands, such as not being able to hold a pen, or with their legs, causing walking or balance issues.

7. Difficulty with mentally processing information from one or more of the five senses (Sensory Processing Disorder [SPD]), such as sensitivity to normal lights or sounds, sensitivity to things, or touching people.

8. Short-term and long-term memory problems, such as a problem with creating or retrieving memories, trouble remembering facts, or instructions.

9. Difficulty understanding what is seen (Visual Processing Disorder [VPD]), not including sight limitations but difficulties understanding and using visual information. For example, the child

may not judge distances well enough, or maybe cannot tell the difference between similar letters.

At any point before your child graduates from high school, you can request that your child be evaluated for learning disabilities. This process takes time because of the many components to it. It can take weeks, if not months, to plan, execute, write the evaluation report, review it, and then schedule a meeting to discuss it. You must also take into account school vacations and breaks.

Ideally, you will prepare your written request three or four months in advance, attaching any reports you have about your child's condition that document what you believe is the disability. This evaluation can happen before kindergarten, or whenever you see your child is having difficulty keeping up. For example, your child may enter the fourth grade and you are concerned that your child's grades, reading level, or whatever, has not been progressing as well as those of other children. It's time for an evaluation if you think there may be a disability interfering with learning.

Once the evaluation is complete, the IEP team will meet with you and discuss the results. At this meeting, a preliminary IEP team might recommend that your child qualifies for special education. If so, the IEP team will draft a plan, which you will review in a team meeting. You will need to sign it before they can implement it.

Your request for an evaluation will give you a good idea of how caring and supportive your local school and school district are.

Here are a few realities not usually told to you:

1. The school has sixty calendar days to follow through with your written request for an evaluation (or your written permission, if a teacher requested the evaluation). However, Federal Laws allow states to set their own time limits, which may allow more time, beyond sixty days.

You need to check your state's rules. You can usually do that through an email or a phone call to a Special Education teacher or the district's Special Education department.

Be mindful of the timing of a request; if a holiday recess, spring break, or summer vacation fall within the sixty-day window, you can expect delays.

2. It will take another few weeks to schedule the meeting where you can discuss the report with teachers and officials, because there are many people to juggle schedules for.

3. The school will put together the "team" that represents the school, but this initial team may not include everyone you will want or need on your child's IEP team.

If your child has a medical diagnosis that is part of the legal definition of learning disability, the school may bypass the formal evaluation process, and an initial meeting might happen sooner. If it doesn't, and if they take the full two months or more allowed, tighten your seatbelt and get ready for a rougher ride through the whole IEP process, because that delay doesn't bode well as a measure of caring and support.

Here is what the written Federal Law (Title 34–Education, Subtitle B, Chapter III, Part 300) says:

A child with a disability means a child evaluated under §§ 300.304 through 300.311 as having: 1. mental retardation, 2. a hearing impairment (including deafness), 3. a speech or language impairment, 4. a visual impairment (including blindness), 5. a serious emotional disturbance, 6. an orthopedic impairment, 7. autism, 8. traumatic brain injury, 9. other health impairment, 10. a specific learning disability, 11. deafness or blindness, or multiple disabilities, 12. and who, by reason thereof, needs special education and related services. (Source: 46756 Federal Register/Vol. 71, No. 156/Monday, August 14, 2006/Rules and Regulations)

Here is a sample letter to request an evaluation to find out if your child qualifies for an IEP:

Today's Date
Your Full Name
Your Street Number and Street Name (and apartment number, if applicable)
City, State, Zip Code
Your Area Code and Telephone Number

Name of Principal or IEP Coordinator
Name of School
School Street Number and Street Name
City, State, Zip Code
Re: Your Child's Full Name
DOB: Your Child's Date of Birth

Dear (Principal's name or IEP Coordinator's name),

My child is in the __ grade, in (name of teacher)'s class at your school. I am writing to request that (your child's name) be evaluated for special education services, under the Child Find obligations of the Individuals with Disabilities Education Act (IDEA).

My child has been struggling with (reading, grades, or whatever), as found in (provide supporting evidence such as test scores, teacher communications, disciplinary issues, examples of work).

I have spoken with the teacher about these concerns and the following things have been tried: (list any interventions that teachers tried, the results, and whatever accommodations they made).

I believe it is critical for my child to be evaluated.

As part of this process, I also ask that you assess (your child's name), under Section 504 of the Rehabilitation Act of 1973, to see whether (s/he) has a disability, as defined by that law.

Please note I am not substituting a 504 assessment for a special education evaluation.

I believe both are appropriate to determine (your child's name)'s needs.

I understand you will send me an evaluation plan explaining the tests.

I will also appreciate receiving any other information you have regarding the evaluation process. If you need more information, please contact me at my phone number.

Thank you very much for your help. I look forward to hearing from you soon.

Sincerely,

Your name

CC: (Name of your child's teacher)

This is how the process was designed to work:

Requests for evaluations or re-evaluations start a sixty-calendar-day clock. (Remember, each state may set a different timeframe.)

After the assessment is completed, school officials will invite you to a meeting, to review and talk about the evaluation results. If the evaluation finds that your child needs special education and related services, then Federal Law insists that a meeting (to develop the IEP) be held within thirty days.

The school will invite you early enough, to ensure you can attend this meeting, and will schedule it at an agreed time and place. If you can't attend in person, you may take part by telephone or a conference call.

After you and the other team members approve the IEP, the law says the school must provide the special education and related services as soon as possible.

A child's IEP needs to be current at the beginning of each school year. The IEP team must review the goals and services, each year. Every three years, a re-evaluation needs to be done, to see if the special education and related services are still needed.

Formal re-evaluations can be dispensed with, if you and the IEP team agree they can be. For example, a student permanently crippled by cerebral palsy (CP) won't be cured, ever. If a student needs special education services because of the CP, this won't ever change.

Every three years, the IEP team may agree to a simple, one-page restatement of the continuing need for special education and an IEP.

SUMMARY CHECKLIST:

1. You, the teachers, or the school officials may request an evaluation to determine if your child qualifies for special education and/or related services. If you are making the request, you need to make it in writing.

2. The process from getting an evaluation to scheduling the first IEP meeting can be very time-consuming, taking from several weeks to over two months, so be patient and understanding.

3. Eligibility for special education requires more than just a disability. Not all disabilities qualify for an IEP. The child must also "need special education" because of the disability, and the school district must agree, for this to take effect.

4. Parents have rights, and one universal right is known as "informed consent." If there is a parent, then Federal Law requires parental consent before the school takes actions affecting the education of minors.

Chapter 3: Who Makes Up the IEP Team?

OVERVIEW:

Federal Laws are clear on the makeup of the IEP team. There is a list of the required members, and then it allows for expanding the team to include whoever else is needed to adequately plan and make it happen.

Unlike sports, where the rules typically spell out the maximum number of players on the field—for example, eleven in American football—for the IEP, the rule spells out the minimum number of team members.

EXPLANATION:

Here are the required team members:

1. The parent(s), including legal guardians. (You are the quarterback, so you lead the team, but you cannot lead a team if you do not join it.)

2. At least one regular education teacher.

3. At least one special education teacher or service provider.

4. At least one school district representative who (a) is qualified to provide or supervise the special education instruction, (b) is knowledgeable about the special education curriculum, and (c) is knowledgeable about district resources.

5. An individual who can interpret the teaching implications of the child's evaluation results.

The law allows any single team member to fill more than one function. For example, a principal may qualify to act as both the school district representative and the interpreter of evaluation results. Another example is that a special education teacher may also be a regular education teacher. However, these should be exceptions rather than the norm and may be more common in smaller schools and districts.

Who else may make up part of your IEP team?

1. Others who know your child or have relevant expertise. For example, the physical education teacher, a tutor, a family member, a minister, a therapist, etc.

2. Your child. The law always considers the student a team member, even if the handicaps or disabilities prevent useful participation. (The law says the student must be invited to attend if the

team is considering the child's transition needs, such as moving into an institution, transitioning from middle to high school, or graduating.)

Who can go with you to an IEP meeting?

You can invite whoever you want. You can bring an attorney, an advocate, or a friend. The law allows you to invite anyone who has knowledge or special expertise about your child. Who you invite may give useful information about your child, or it might be somebody who will provide moral support for you. You decide who meets those criteria.

It's always a good idea to notify the school in advance that you will be bringing someone with you. This can be done when you respond to the school's prior written notice (PWN) to you scheduling the IEP meeting. You will let them know you plan on attending, that you will be bringing a guest, and who that guest is.

If you are bringing an attorney to represent your child, consider it mandatory that you notify the school.

If you bring a lawyer, some districts will insist they bring their own to the meeting. If you spring it on them the day of the meeting, expect them to cancel that meeting and insist on rescheduling.

Whoever you bring will take a supportive, helping role. They won't be expected to take over for you.

Our own story is an example. Our first IEP team meeting was held when our granddaughter, who we were raising, turned three years old in January. We'll call her Jill, although that's not her real name. Her Medicaid covered physical therapy (PT), occupational therapy (OT), and speech and vision therapies, which were to be supplied through the school system.

At the time, we did not understand what IEPs were. We sat through a friendly meeting (our first), where we listened to what we were told Jill needed and that she would join a pre-kindergarten special education program for three-year-olds and four-year-olds.

Jill joined the program, blossomed, and thoroughly enjoyed it. Two months shy of her fifth birthday, we were summoned to a third IEP team meeting by the school district's Department of Special Education. At that meeting, we were told Jill had to leave the program—in mid-year—when she turned five. We objected, we argued, we pleaded, and we yelled that she should be allowed to finish out the school year while we looked into other programs. The district representative was stone-cold adamant that would not happen; our granddaughter had to leave the program. There was no flexibility; no negotiating. We left that meeting feeling exasperated, announcing that we would homeschool her instead.

We had once-a-week, thirty-minute visits from therapists and a special education teacher. There were no interactions with children her own age. After a year of this, we knew homeschooling wasn't the answer for our granddaughter, and we notified the district we wanted to enroll her in kindergarten in the fall. We were told a school psychologist would have to come to the house and assess her, for placement decisions.

We had been teaching Jill for a year, reading to her, helping her learn the alphabet, the colors, and numbers (one to ten). We knew she was intelligent, despite her cerebral palsy. Jill could not sit, walk, crawl, or eat solid foods. She could not speak at all, but she could communicate by pointing with the one hand she had some control over, by grunts and squeals, and by facial expressions.

The school psychologist arrived and administered a verbal IQ test to our nonverbal child. The psychologist reported that Jill could not be taught; that Jill could not learn. This was based on the fact that Jill had not given a single answer to any of the ninety questions asked. The psychologist refused to accept Jill's pointing and gesturing as answers because the standardized test required verbal answers.

We knew that was an invalid assessment—giving an oral test to a nonverbal child was ridiculous and wrong—and if we didn't challenge it, Jill would be denied a free, public education.

We did two things before the IEP meeting that would determine Jill's fate in the school system:

1. We got a speech-generating laptop that Jill could use to speak for herself.

2. We engaged an attorney to represent her interests. This attorney prepared us by explaining education laws to us, as best as he could. Incidentally, he was free to us through a non-profit organization that served disabled persons.

We notified the school that the attorney would attend the IEP team meeting. The district responded by including the district's attorney and the District Director for Special Education.

You should expect similar reactions when you bring supporters to your meeting. Other than introducing herself at the beginning of the IEP team meeting, Jill's attorney didn't have to say another word. She didn't have to speak because Jill did.

Jill used her laptop and speech-generating app to prove to the team she was intelligent, able to learn, and able to communicate. She generated a short message: "Hello. My name is Jill."

The Director of Special Education, a Ph.D. responsible for the entire school district special education program, stopped the meeting right there and publicly apologized to us, admitting they had made a serious mistake with that IQ test.

We've had almost two dozen IEP team meetings since then.

Over the last decade, I read everything I could find about special education laws. I went to training programs put on by the Wrightslaw firm. I eventually got my paralegal diploma.

I've never experienced another contentious IEP meeting.

I don't have to fight the school district anymore, because I know the laws. As I mentioned in the introduction, knowledge is power. I now have the knowledge and power to manage my granddaughter's IEP team, to make sure it is a team working for her and her best interests.

After reading this book (and the rest of the books in this series), you will have that knowledge, too.

SUMMARY CHECKLIST:

1. There are five required team members; but remember, one person may wear more than one hat.

2. You (the parent) must be included in the team. In fact, you are essential to the team.

3. You may bring anyone with you to IEP meetings that you want, for help or support.

4. It's standard and polite to notify the school that you will be bringing someone, especially if it is an attorney.

5. Think of your child's IEP team as getting on the team bus to travel to an event. You are in the driver's seat. Just like a bus driver doesn't need to be a mechanic to drive, you don't need to be a lawyer to know how to drive this team. However, just like a bus driver needs to know about legal traffic laws, you need to know enough about special education laws to be an effective advocate for your child.

Chapter 4: Preparing for Your First IEP Meeting

OVERVIEW:

The first meeting after an assessment of handicaps and disabilities is held to discuss the results and to decide if the student qualifies for an IEP.

The focus is on whether or not the school district agrees and an IEP is needed for your child, but if the needs are so clear and evident to everyone, the focus will shift to actually defining what special accommodations will be provided.

Before the meeting, prepare notes about what you want to learn or find out at the meeting. Ask for copies of any school evaluations done, a week before the meeting. Prepare notes about what you want your child to learn in school.

EXPLANATION:

1. The first actual IEP team meeting is held to design the initial IEP, to define what special services are needed, to set goals, and to set progress reporting schedules.

2. Interim meetings may be held to discuss progress and whether adjustments in the program are needed.

3. The annual review meeting reviews the prior year's goals, the progress attained, and designs the following year's program.

4. Resolution meetings or behavior problem meetings may be held, if there are conflicts, disagreements, or behavioral issues that occur. These are like interim meetings, but typically are tinged with more problem-solving and negotiation (including disagreements) than an interim meeting might have.

5. Transition IEP meetings are held, before major changes in placement or graduation.

Someone requested an evaluation of your child—maybe you, maybe a teacher, or perhaps a school therapist—to see if your child qualifies for a special education program. You gave your consent, school specialists did the evaluation, and now it's time to meet to review and discuss the findings and the evaluation report. This is the first meeting, listed above.

During this meeting, you can expect to mostly listen to the report. Be prepared to ask over and over for explanations and clarifications about what the results mean for your child. Use the questioning strategy of "If this were your child...?" to discover their goals, motives, and rationales, so you can understand the school's position. If you don't understand something, say, "I don't know what you mean, so can you clarify that, please?" Remain calm and demonstrate confidence and competence. After all, it's your child that the team is making decisions for!

Also, be prepared for one of three outcomes:

1. Your child doesn't meet the definition of having a disability and will attend general education classes.

2. Your child has a disability, but it doesn't interfere with the child's educational progress, so your child will not have an IEP. There may be the need for a 504 Plan. (Refer to Chapter 1 for the differences between the two plans.)

3. Your child has a disability that interferes with learning, and an IEP customized to your child's circumstances needs to be created and followed.

If you disagree with the findings in the first two outcomes, what comes next is beyond the scope of this book and will be addressed in a later book in this series. When you disagree, you need to start an appeal process, first through the school system, as you won't yet be at a level where you need to involve the courts.

For now, we will address the third outcome.

Let's assume the school district agrees your child has one or more disabilities and needs a special education program because of these disabilities. The IEP team will meet to design the first IEP. This may occur during the meeting where the evaluation was discussed, or it might occur in a follow-up meeting that includes the teachers, therapists, and specialists the evaluation report said should be included on the IEP team.

What should happen during the first IEP meeting?

The discussion should really focus on just a few topics:

• your child's present strengths

• your child's present areas of need

• addressing the areas of need by drafting measurable goals

• deciding upon specially designed instruction (SDI) adaptations needed to meet these goals

• extended school year (ESY)—summer school—eligibility

• focused behavioral intervention methods and behavior plans (if relevant)

• how progress will be measured and when it will be reported to you

That's it. So, you can see from that list, if you took part in the evaluation portion of the IEP process, there should be no (or very few) surprises.

Meetings are typically held in a conference room (that can hold a big table and all the chairs, and perhaps several desks or counters that line some walls, acting like storage surfaces for files, a printer, and a copier), or maybe it will be in an empty classroom. Usually, there is some sort of conference table. I have always had to wait in the school's lobby while watching teachers, therapists, and vice principals walk in and get settled before I'm escorted in. (I get to watch this because my rule is to be there at least ten minutes before the scheduled starting time.)

There will be a crowd of at least six people sitting around the table, although it's usually closer to ten. When you enter, you will likely recognize the special education teacher who you've met previously when touring the school; you might also have met one or two others. Most are strangers, but they all look very professional and managerial. There are suits and ties, dresses or pant suits, and maybe one athletic sweat suit—on the PE teacher. There will also likely be an overhead projector on the table, pointing at a screen toward the far end. Remember, you can bring someone along as a source of support.

The person chairing the meeting may be a vice principal (if it is the first meeting), the school psychologist (if assessment results are the main issues), or the special education teacher. The chairperson will start the meeting by having each person introduce themselves by name and position or function. You will introduce yourself. The meeting is usually scheduled during the workday, and is allotted thirty to sixty minutes, so everyone is feeling rushed.

During the IEP meeting, the different members of the IEP team will share their thoughts and suggestions. If this is the first IEP meeting after your child's evaluation, the team may go over the evaluation results. At every IEP meeting, your child's current strengths and needs—both academic and functional—should be addressed first. These will help the team focus on what special help your child needs. Look for opportunities to express gratitude to teachers and related staff, to show your appreciation to them for looking out for the best interests of your child.

After the various team members (including you) have shared their thoughts and concerns, the group will have a better idea of your child's strengths and shortfalls. This will allow the team to discuss and decide on the statements associated with each IEP's component, especially the "present levels" statement, the educational and other goals appropriate for your child, and which related services are necessary to help your child benefit from special education.

The IEP team will probably spend most of the time focused on how your child's needs can be addressed, through written goals and the special education and related services appropriate for your child.

The team must also decide about whether any of the "special factors" identified in the Individuals with Disabilities Act (IDEA) need to be considered, including the child's needs for assistive technology. These might include tablet computers, tape recorders, wheelchairs, lifting devices, and so on.

Depending on your child's needs, the IEP team may also discuss special factors, such as the following situations:

1. If your child's behaviors will interfere with their learning or the learning of others, the team

will talk about strategies and supports to address your child's behavior.

2. If your child has a limited proficiency in English, the team will talk about your child's language needs and perhaps extra tutoring.

3. If your child is blind or visually impaired, the IEP team must provide for instruction in Braille or the use of Braille, unless it determines, after an appropriate evaluation, that your child does not need Braille.

4. If your child has communication needs, the team must consider how to adjust for this, including the need to provide speech-generating devices, communication boards, and maybe even sign language instruction.

5. If your child is deaf or hard of hearing, the IEP team will consider your child's language and communication needs. This includes opportunities to communicate directly with classmates and school staff in the usual method of communication (for example, sign language). The school may also need to provide special display tools to enhance your child's reading ability.

If any of these adaptations require specialized training for teachers, therapists, or parents,

Federal Laws require the school provide that— FREE of charge to you.

If you are compromising, define how and when to evaluate if the compromise is working.

Note that you can ask for additional time to consider important decisions, if you're uncomfortable making them on the spot at the meeting or want to get additional input.

SUMMARY CHECKLIST:

1. Know your rights. Know the rules. Knowledge is power!

2. Prepare notes about what you want to learn or find out at the meeting.

3. A week before the meeting, ask for copies of any school evaluations done.

4. Prepare notes about what you want your child to learn in school.

5. Bring someone along as a source of support.

6. Remain calm.

7. Look for opportunities to express gratitude to teachers and related staff.

8. Use the questioning strategy of "If this were your child…?" Don't blame or criticize. Instead,

ask questions to discover their goals, motives, and rationales. You want to understand the school's position.

9. Saying "I don't know what you mean" is a demonstration of confidence and competence.

10. At the meeting, feel free to ask for additional time to consider important decisions, if you're uncomfortable making them on the spot, or if you want to get additional input from people not present (such as your lawyer or other family members).

11. If compromising, define how and when to evaluate if the compromise is working.

Chapter 5: The Ideal IEP Template

OVERVIEW:

The U.S. Department of Education has published a guide to help parents and schools design a good IEP. This template is more than a mere suggestion because it actually sets out the minimum standards needed to comply with the law. It is your benchmark.

EXPLANATION:

The Individualized Education Program is a written document. It is developed for each child with a disability that qualifies for an IEP.

These are the required items to be included in an IEP:

◆ First and most important, the law requires a statement of your child's present levels of academic achievement and functional performance. This includes how your child's disability will affect their participation in the general education curriculum. (For preschool children, this includes how the disability affects the child's participation in appropriate activities.)

◆ Statements of measurable, annual goals, including both academic and functional goals designed to meet your child's needs so your child can be involved in and make progress in the general education curriculum as much as possible AND meet each of the other educational needs arising from your child's disability.

◆ An outline that will advance appropriately toward attaining the annual goals and a description of how you and your child's teachers will measure progress toward meeting the measurable, annual goals.

◆ The transition services (including courses of study) needed to assist your child in reaching those goals.

◆ A description of the benchmarks or short-term objectives, for children who take alternate assessments and alternate achievement standards (in addition to the annual goals).

◆ A statement that outlines when the school will provide periodic progress reports (for example, quarterly reports at the same time as report cards are issued), because parents must be able to track how their child is making progress.

◆ A statement of the special education and/or related services, the supplementary aids that are to be provided to your child, and the modifications or supports for school teachers and therapists that will be provided to help your child.

◆ The date when services and modifications will start, the frequency at which they will occur, the location where they will occur, and the duration of special services and other aids, services, modifications, and supports.

◆ A statement that says how your child will be involved in and make progress in the general education curriculum as well as how your child will engage in extracurricular and other non-academic activities, including an explanation of the extent to which your child will not take part with nondisabled children in the regular classroom and in extracurricular and other non-academic activities.

◆ A statement of any accommodations necessary to measure academic achievement and functional performance on State and districtwide tests.

◆ If the IEP Team determines the child must take an alternate assessment instead of a particular regular State or districtwide assessment of student achievement, then the IEP needs to include a statement of why the child can't participate in the regular assessment AND a statement of why the alternate assessment selected is appropriate.

◆ Beginning not later than the first IEP, to be in effect when your child turns 16—or younger if determined appropriate by the IEP Team—and updated every year after that, the IEP must include: (1) appropriate and measurable postsecondary goals related to training, education, employment, and where appropriate, independent living skills, based upon age-appropriate assessments, AND (2) rights that transfer when your child reaches adult age.

◆ Beginning not later than one year before your child reaches the age of majority under State law (that is, becomes of legal age), the IEP must include a statement that you and your child have been informed of the adult rights that will transfer to your child.

SUMMARY CHECKLIST:

The Federal requirements for the contents of the IEP are straightforward, saying that an Individualized Education Program for each child must include:

1. A description of your child's present levels of educational performance.

2. A statement of annual goals, including short-term instructional objectives.

3. The specific special education and related services to be provided to your child, and the extent to which your child will take part in regular educational programs.

4. Beginning no later than age 16, the transition services your child needs, including, if appropriate, a statement of each public agency's and each participating agency's responsibilities before your child leaves the school setting.

5. The projected dates for initiation of services and the expected duration of the services.

6. Appropriate objective criteria and evaluation procedures and schedules for determining, whether the short-term instructional objectives are being achieved.

DAVID SOFI

Chapter 6: What Happens After the Meeting?

OVERVIEW:

The IEP meeting sort of ends when everyone leaves the meeting room. I say "sort of" because there remain two vital closing steps. First, you must receive a signed copy of the IEP. This may be handed to you right then at the school, or it might be sent to you later. Second, you need to review the printed, final version to make sure it is what you expected. Only then does the meeting really end.

EXPLANATION:

Depending on how your school handles the IEP paperwork, you will receive a copy of the final plan either at the end of the meeting, or after it is reviewed by a district representative charged with the job of making sure the IEP meets Federal regulations.

It may take a week (or perhaps two weeks) before you receive the final, printed plan. If you haven't received it after ten school days following the meeting, it's time to pester the school, in writing.

During your meeting, a school representative may say they want to send you a clean, final copy later. Politely make it clear you want a copy of the original or the draft of IEP before you leave the meeting. Ask that they send you the final copy when it's available.

When you get the final copy, compare it to the original.

Once you receive the final version, read it over carefully to make sure the minutes and the wording are what you heard and agreed to.

1. Does the IEP include accurate information about your child's present levels of academic achievement and functional performance?

2. Does the IEP identify all of your child's needs that result from the disability?

3. Does the IEP include measurable goals?

4. Does the IEP describe how and when the school will measure your child's progress toward the goals?

5. Does the IEP specify when you will receive reports on your child's progress toward the annual goals?

6. Does the IEP include a statement of the special education services, related services, and

supplementary aids and services that the school will provide?

7. Does the IEP allow your child to make progress in the general curriculum and take part in extracurricular and other non-academic activities?

8. Does the IEP explain the extent to which your child will be educated with children who are not disabled?

9. Does the IEP include the projected date services will begin? The frequency? The location and duration of services?

You will get periodic progress reports. Put reminders on your calendar of the dates you can expect those reports. Don't skip them.

When you receive them, read them carefully.

For each goal, ask yourself if the progress report shows if your child is falling behind, meeting, or advancing beyond schedule.

If your child is off the schedule (either falling behind or skipping ahead), then you should talk with the teachers about possibly changing the plan.

Document everything and write to the IEP team leader after EVERY meeting!

One habit you should develop is writing down all communications you have with school employees about your child's education.

You will, someday, need to go into a meeting to advocate or negotiate, on behalf of your child. Your chances of walking away feeling like a success will be ten times greater if you walk in with written records of who said what, when, and why.

Additionally, after every IEP meeting, you should document—in a letter or an email—your belief and understanding of what was discussed, what decisions were made, and who has any follow-up actions to take.

Let me repeat this: there is one important, necessary thing that YOU MUST DO after every IEP meeting: write a letter to your IEP team leader.

Remember, in IEP land, it is all about the paper trail. Follow the tenet that if you didn't write it down, it didn't happen.

When and how should you write such a letter?

Within 24-48 hours after your IEP meeting, write a letter that begins similar to the following:

Dear (name of special education team leader),

Thank you and the team for meeting with me today to discuss (name of child). A lot of information was presented and discussed, so I want to make sure I have everything correct.

As I recall, we discussed:

* List what was discussed—EVERY SINGLE ITEM—and bullet-point them, for simplicity).

* List items you are not happy with. For example: "We discussed the possibility of getting Jacob one-to-one support with _____, which most of the team disagreed with, but I still feel he needs."

* List items you are unsure about. For example, "We discussed increasing his OT from once per week to twice per week, but we did not discuss when that will begin. Please make sure that is clarified on the IEP."

End your letter with sentences that are similar to the following:

"Please let me know if I have forgotten anything or misunderstood anything. I will look for my finalized copy of the IEP within the next week."

This is simple and it puts the ball in their court. If they refute nothing that you have said, in the eyes of the law, it stands as truth. You have let them know that you expect a signed IEP with all the items on it, and you were not confrontational about it. If the IEP arrives with missing items, or items on it that differ from what was discussed, you have written data to refute it.

SUMMARY CHECKLIST:

1. Get a copy of the IEP draft at the end of the meeting, if they are providing a final copy later.

2. Write a polite letter to the IEP team within a couple of days after the meeting, thanking them, listing your beliefs and understandings of what was discussed, and noting what you agreed or disagreed with. Remember to leave the ball in their court by ending your letter with a question or a statement that prompts them to respond to you.

3. Read the final IEP carefully to ensure you agree with the wording.

4. Put reminders on your calendar of the dates you can expect progress reports.

5. Follow up religiously on progress reports, documenting with follow-up emails or letters.

6. Document everything! Remember the tenet that "If it isn't written, it didn't happen, and it wasn't said."

Conclusion

You should now have a clearer understanding of what an IEP is; how you get one; what the laws say an IEP should contain; how an IEP differs from a Section 504 Plan; who makes up the IEP team; how you should prepare for your first IEP meeting; what to do before, during, and after your first IEP meeting; and some of the laws that govern you and your special needs child.

The rest of this book series will cover many more topics, including: how so use the law to make special requests (and be approved for them), the law and disciplinary issues, troubleshooting district problems with IEPs, IEPs and private schools, how to track your child's progress, the law and school activities, the law and assistive technology, the law and non-academic issues, IEPs and the school board, and if your child's school must provide training for you.

These are issues all parents, guardians, and caregivers of special needs children need to know!

I look forward to helping you navigate your way through these topics and empowering you with the knowledge and confidence you need to ensure your child's IEP is the best one possible!

About the Author

DAVID SOFI was born and raised in the United States of America. He currently lives in South Carolina, the ninth state he has called "home." He has been a pharmaceutical executive, a corporate consultant, a government security contractor, and a paralegal. He spearheaded the first breast cancer drug allowed to use the word "cure" and was a first responder to 911 medical emergencies, as a paramedic.

David Sofi is a widower. He and his late wife both raised his special needs granddaughter. He is still a caregiver to her. Over the course of ten years, he learned the hard way how to use special education laws to get the free education owed to this child. He first ran into a hard-nosed school district official whose stubbornness forced him to pull his granddaughter out of school for home schooling. After a year of that, he wanted her to go to school with her peers. The district tried to warehouse her in a profoundly disabled classroom, using a standardized psychological test requiring spoken answers, even though his granddaughter cannot speak due to having cerebral palsy. The psychologist said she was "trainable" but not "educable."

David Sofi enlisted the help of a pro bono attorney and a speech-generating app for her pre-kindergarten IEP. The district officials immediately apologized for their mistakes.

David Sofi saw the power that the IEP laws give to parents, if only they can understand the legalese. For five years, he squashed problems before they arose. He got his grandchild a one-to-one aide (a shadow) and he got her two iPads, when the district issued only one to other students. He made sure she was included and enjoyed all field trips and sports, with special accommodations made for her.

David Sofi earned a paralegal diploma because he saw that he could help other families by becoming an expert in reading the special education laws and translating the laws to parents and guardians of special needs children. He is now on a mission to help them conquer the same hurdles he faced but without the frustrations and long study nights he endured.

This is the first book in the "IEPs for Children with Special Needs" series.